VITAMINS
FOR THE
SOUL

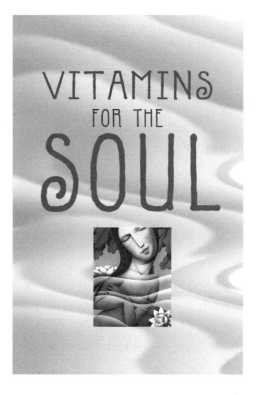

OTHER HAY HOUSE TITLES
BY SONIA CHOQUETTE

Ask Your Guides Oracle Cards

Diary of a Psychic

Soul Lessons and Soul Purpose Cards
(available January 2006)

Trust Your Vibes

Trust Your Vibes Oracle Cards

VITAMINS
FOR THE
SOUL
DAILY DOSES OF WISDOM
FOR PERSONAL EMPOWERMENT

SONIA CHOQUETTE

HAY HOUSE, INC.
Carlsbad, California
London • Sydney • Johannesburg
Vancouver • New Delhi

Published and distributed in the United States by: Hay House, Inc.: www.hayhouse.com • **Published and distributed in Australia by:** Hay House Australia Pty. Ltd.: www.hayhouse.com.au • **Published and distributed in the United Kingdom by:** Hay House UK, Ltd.: www.hayhouse.co.uk • **Published and distributed in the Republic of South Africa by:** Hay House SA (Pty), Ltd.: orders@psd-prom.co.za • **Distributed in Canada by:** Raincoast: www.raincoast.com • **Published in India by:** Hay House Publications (India) Pvt. Ltd.: www.hayhouseindia.co.in • **Distributed in India by:** Media Star: booksdivision@mediastar.co.in

Editorial supervision: Jill Kramer   Design: Amy Rose Szalkiewicz

Library of Congress Control Number: 2004115050

ISBN 13: 978-1-4019-0540-8
ISBN 10: 1-4019-0540-4

09   08   07   06   6   5   4   3

1st printing, April 2005
3rd printing, June 2006

Printed in Canada

INTRODUCTION

Each time you choose to listen to your inner voice (or your sixth sense), you strengthen your commitment to live an authentic, self-directed, and personally empowered life. Your inner voice is communicated through subtle vibrations pulsating throughout your body, otherwise known as "vibes."

Trusting your vibes relieves you of the stress of figuring things out—it saves you the wear and tear of worry and helps you begin living a life of ease and flow. Listening to your inner voice reflects your commitment to live a six-sensory life—the one you were designed to live as a Divine Child of the Universe. Just as taking vitamins strengthens and empowers your body, trusting your vibes strengthens and empowers your soul. Yet, as you know, just occasionally popping a multivitamin won't do you much good—in the same way, it's only when you trust your vibes on a daily basis over time that you'll begin to feel, see, and experience a positive and powerful difference in your life.

Like vitamins for the soul, trusting your vibes strengthens your spirit, enhances your creativity, improves your decision-making abilities; and helps you become a more empowered, joyful, and healthy person. Every time you choose to do so, you give your soul a dose of love and acceptance. These daily doses heal your heart and restore you to a brighter, happier existence.

Learning to trust your vibes is possible, but if you want to see a real difference in your life, you must make it a habit. Consider each page in this book a daily fortification for your soul—that is, one page should be consulted every day. Open the book at random, and take the offering on that page as your "vitamin"—you'll soon discover that the wisdom you receive is perfect for that day. The synchronicity will be undeniable, and the results, if you take your psychic vitamins regularly, will speak for themselves.

If you're under particular stress or in need of a megadose of psychic guidance, simply open the book as often as needed and follow the instructions therein. Each page offers you another shot of soul food for personal power and peace of mind, which will make trusting your vibes a matter of habit.

And if you take your psychic vitamins every day, you'll definitely experience a change: You'll go from living a fear-based, five-sensory, average life, to a heart-based, six-sensory, extraordinary life—one that restores your true voice, frees your spirit, and leads you at all times to the best possible outcomes. You'll soon see, feel, and experience the magic it brings.

VITAMINS
FOR THE
SOUL

"I AM . . ."

Did you know that the words *I am* . . . are very powerful metaphysical words? Whenever you say "I am," you proclaim who you are and want to be to the Universe, to others, and to yourself—and the Universe agrees and makes it so. That's why it's so damaging to make proclamations such as: "I am unhappy," "I am broke," "I am sick," "I am fat," or "I am unlovable." These statements absolutely attract such unpleasant conditions. This week, use the power mantra "I am . . . " to create the exact conditions you want in your life.

Try these affirmations:

- "I am healthy."
- "I am balanced."
- "I am happily employed."
- "I am loved and lovable."
- "I am beautiful."
- "I am a prosperous, creative being."
- "I am joyful, lighthearted, and blessed in every way."

BEGIN WITH GRACE

The Chinese have a saying: "The way it begins is the way it ends."

Begin your new project by affirming: "I am a spiritual being, protected by angels, helped by guides, and infinitely loved and supported by God."

TEN WAYS
TO NURTURE YOUR SPIRIT

1. When you leave work, really *leave work*.

2. Go for a walk with someone you love.

3. Invite friends over for a potluck dinner, followed by an evening of board games.

4. Unplug the phone during dinner.

5. Don't take work calls in the evening or on weekends.

6. Tell stories instead of watching TV.

7. Play with your pet.

8. Do something creative or artistic with your hands, and give your mind a rest.

9. Write a long letter to a loved one.

10. Take a leisurely bubble bath while reading your favorite magazine.

LISTEN TO YOUR HIGHER SELF

Listen to your Higher Self over everything else: It will naturally guide you to what it is you really need for change and serenity.

When you commit to living the six-sensory life, you begin your spiritual healing. You'll recover your childlike joy, you'll be able to love yourself in a deep and profound way, and you'll start to feel how magnificent you really are.

YOU DECIDE

Making the decision to trust your vibes is definitely a healing experience. . . .

Ask your Higher Self to help you in your new commitment. Approach your changes with a sense of humor and playfulness. Don't worry about whether or not your vibes are "right"—just listen for what's true for you for now. And go with it (that's the hardest part).

BE FLEXIBLE

Be flexible.

The more adjustable you are, the more your Higher Self can guide you. And be physical about it: Get out of your head. Dance as much as you can. Stretch! Bend! Twist!

WRITE TO
YOUR HIGHER SELF

Here's an exciting tool for contacting your Higher Self when you need guidance: Write your Higher Self a letter, asking for help on whatever matter concerns you, and then imagine that your Higher Self is answering you.

As easy as this is, it works. By simply opening the way for your Higher Self to communicate, it will. You'll be amazed by the bright ideas, suggestions, and solutions that come pouring through your pen.

It's even better to make this a daily practice, as doing so allows your inner genius to go to work for you in virtually every way.

COUNT YOUR BLESSINGS

How has your Higher Self helped you this week? What gifts from your "inner teacher" have you received? Are you enjoying this whole new way of life? Are you starting to notice just how fun it is to go with the flow and trust your vibes instead of resisting?

Do you like having the Universe on your side?

IT'S IN THE HEART

We find our inner voice and the path to personal joy in the heart. It leads the way to a broader, deeper perspective and understanding of both ourselves and others. It brings our attention to the unseen subtle aspects of life and directs us toward a more creative, more loving, and more healing approach to the difficulties that arise.

TAKE A DEEP BREATH

Every time you need guidance, counsel, direction, or simple reassurance from Divine Spirit, close your eyes, take in a few deep-cleansing breaths, and then place your attention directly on your heart.

Allow your focus to rest there quietly for a moment or two, and then ask your heart to guide you. Trust whatever feelings come up—don't censor or discount a thing.

If nothing comes to you immediately, don't worry. Relax. Remain open and patient. Guidance will come before you know it.

INSTANT RELIEF

Listening to your heart and following your vibes will instill in you a profound sense of confidence and security. It isn't an assurance that arises from an egotistical sense of "I'm so wonderful"—rather, it's a sense of relief, knowing that you don't have to do it on your own. You only have to do your part, and the Universe will meet you halfway with support, protection, and guidance.

A HAND ON YOUR HEART

A great way to open your heart is to actually place your hand over it. Let it rest there as you speak and listen to another person. This gesture indicates that you're sharing your deepest truth and that you want to be honestly heard. It also conveys that you're truly willing to listen to another as well.

This is an especially effective technique for settling arguments and opening up troubled communication. It clears away discord and allows real understanding and communication to occur.

TRUST WHAT YOU FEEL

Peace of mind and personal joy come from paying as much attention to the nonphysical dimensions of who you are as you do to the physical dimensions. This means acknowledging your vibes as readily as you do green lights and stop signs. It comes from noticing whenever anything is "off" on any level, and choosing to listen to your vibes so that you can make changes that will bring you back into balance.

It's only when you trust your heart—by responding to these signals and acting on your instincts—that your spirit will remain on course and move in the right direction.

TAKE RESPONSIBILITY

Your intuition is a gift, but in order to fully experience it, you must take responsibility for it. This means that you realize your sixth sense isn't something that others may necessarily support. You must be willing to walk through the gate of self-direction by yourself, out of the ordinary world and into that of the extraordinary. Once through, you'll find others like yourself, but as you approach such a liberated life, you'll definitely feel alone.

The words on the door into the world of the extraordinary are: "Enter only if you're willing to take full responsibility for yourself." If you choose to begin your six-sensory life in this way, you'll be met with miracles, magic, and the companionship of other truly amazing and powerful helpers.

TRUST YOUR VIBES

True intention, the natural voice of your Higher Self, seeks only to make your life better. You can trust it to guide and help you in every way. Practice trusting your vibes, even when it's challenging or difficult. Be willing to give up your old, fixed perceptions and beliefs. Haven't you noticed that they don't work anyway?

Become spontaneous, flexible, and open to redirecting yourself midstream if your Higher Self suggests that you do so. Trusting your Higher Self will change the way you are in the world. It may feel difficult at first, but what you experience will only be relief.

❀

LOOK AT THE STARS!

Noticing your intuition is like noticing stars: For the longest time you can go along never seeing the dark sky overhead, then one night you look up and are aware of sparkling stars above you. Taken by their lovely twinkle, you become drawn into the blackness, seeking more bright "skylights." At first you may see only a few, then more, then still more, until quite spontaneously your whole perception shifts—and suddenly the sky seems to explode with thousands upon thousands of stars.

It's humbling to realize that although these lights were in the sky all along, you're just seeing them for the first time.

ALLOW YOURSELF TO WONDER

An exciting way to activate your intuition is through wonder.

This feeling of amazement sets the tone for your spirit to guide you. It gets you out of your head and takes you into your creative and playful heart. It invites you to explore the unseen world with enthusiasm and open-mindedness. It helps you access the unknown, spiritual, and resourceful side of life . . . and of yourself.

Wonder directs your attention to options that you might have otherwise overlooked, and it keeps your awareness fresh and keen. And the best part is that it's fun!

NOW, WONDER . . .

. . . who's calling when the phone
   rings.

. . . where you'll find a parking space.

. . . when the elevator will come.

. . . who people really are instead of
   judging them by appearance.

. . . how to do your best work instead
   of falling into a rut.

. . . what your real talents are.

. . . what your heart's desires are.

CLEAR THE NEGATIVITY

Here are other ways to keep your energy clear and your intuitive spirit singing:

- Avoid emotionally charged situations.

- Wait until you're calm and centered before checking in with your vibes.

- Avoid setting up "tests" when it comes to intuition.

- Be curious, not controlling.

- Allow yourself to explore without censoring yourself. If your vibes are wrong, say, "Oh, well," instead of, "Oh, no!"

- When your intuition serves you, openly acknowledge it— and celebrate!

WALK WITH
A GENTLE HEART

If you honor your intuitive soul, you walk with a gentle, joyous heart—the heart of a child.

BE OPEN
TO DIVINE GUIDANCE

Be open to receiving Divine guidance every day—this is the first step to living a six-sensory life.

Making this choice will allow you to benefit immediately. It's the key to being assisted by the Universe, including your angels, your guides, your Higher Self, and God. Don't continue to do things in the old, difficult, five-sensory way . . . do them in the more creative and effective six-sensory way!

PAY ATTENTION TO YOUR VIBES

Pay attention to your vibes. Notice where they arise in your body: Do they resonate in your gut? In your head? In your throat? All over? All under?

Noticing will put you in touch with your authentic self and help you express that in your life. So notice what your vibes are telling you . . . and trust them!

BELIEVE IN YOUR SPIRIT

The greatest catalyst to living in a higher way is to simply believe you can. Belief pulls back the curtain of fear and allows you to see the truth.

Try this: Pretend for one day that you're a magician—you can create exactly what you want easily, painlessly, and with grace and style. What will you create?

FIND YOUR COURAGE

Living the six-sensory life takes courage. It isn't easy to let go of the egocentric messages that say you're made up only of body and mind, and that your worth is defined by the opinions and feedback of others. Trusting your vibes escorts you out of the "land of the old" and invites you to live in a new way—one that follows the counsel of your Higher Self, your angels, and guides; is receptive to miracles; and is willing to be helped at every given moment. The new way recognizes that you're a beautiful soul who's protected, loved, and guided every step along your path.

Are you willing to approach your life in this new way?

CHANGE YOUR ATTITUDE

At some point it may be necessary to change your attitude and your perspective. So wake up and smell the coffee if you haven't been paying attention!

Take off the rose-colored glasses, snap out of denial, and change your plans when called for. Be glad that you have a sixth sense to keep your life safe, balanced, and happy—and *use* it!

INHALE . . .

. . . let the Universe support you.

GET A NEW STORY

Living a six-sensory life will give you a new perspective on old issues and emotions and ask you to draw new conclusions.

In other words, leave the "old story" behind and get a new one, which reflects the person you want to be today. It's possible, even likely, that you may encounter resistance from others as you set about to bring new conditions and responses into your life—be prepared, and resist their attempts to sabotage you.

The best way to do so is to keep your spirit strong and well cared for. Be discreet; don't invite attack or challenge; and give your body a healthy diet, get plenty of sleep, exercise every day, and have fun. All these things ground your spirit, strengthen your soul, and help keep you true to yourself.

OLD STORY:

"I don't know where I'm going, and I don't know what I'm doing, but I sure hope it works out."

"My experience is better, happier, and more productive when I trust my vibes. I don't need approval from others—my success in life is my approval."

AVOID DRAMA

Avoid unnecessary turmoil as you embrace your six-sensory life—that is, don't try to convert anyone to your brighter, more enlightened point of view. Following your vibes allows you to operate in the world with more ease and flow, but you must use this channel with discretion.

Start off easily and in small, non-threatening ways. Then as you develop confidence in your vibes, you can gradually expand into more and more arenas. Ask your Higher Self to help you in every possible way to succeed in your goals. The Universe wants to help. Let it.

LOOK FOR WHAT'S TRUE

If you want to live the six-sensory life, then you must choose to look at life and respond to it differently. Don't look for what's "right" or "wrong"—look instead for what feels true for you . . . for now. And go with it.

Know in your heart that you're being helped by your guides, your Higher Self, and God with each experience you face, no matter how difficult. And remember: *Six-sensory people live in trust and faith!*

LET YOUR HIGHER SELF LEAD

Allow the Universe to guide you . . . let things come to you in a completely new and different way.

A six-sensory life is exciting! It brings all sorts of new opportunities, new perspectives, and new ways of achieving your goals directly to your doorstep. It invites in creativity, support, and genius. Moment by magical moment, it seeks only to create the life you really want.

LISTEN TO YOUR HIGHER SELF, NOT TO OTHERS

As you begin to awaken spiritually (listening to your Higher Self instead of others), you'll be able to act on, rather than merely *re*act to, the conditions around you.

When you honor your vibes, your intuition gives you a spiritual power that you may have never experienced before. It will allow you to feel more confidence and competence about your decisions, and it will lead to the best possible outcomes in all your endeavors.

NURTURE
YOUR AUTHENTIC SELF

One thing you'll discover when you begin to activate your sixth sense is that what you're truly doing is nurturing your most authentic self, your spirit. Nurturing intuition is actually the art of discovering and honoring who you really are.

FOLLOW YOUR VIBES

Following your vibes introduces you to a world that's friendly, adventurous, and amusing—but most of all, it's one that welcomes your unique soul. It invites you to experience real power in your life, which comes from within and can't be diminished by anyone.

SET YOUR INTENTION

No matter what you want to create, the Universe wants to help. However, it won't work harder than you in bringing about your intentions because that would override your greatest gift: your free will.

Once you set your intention, though, the Universe joins in! As you move toward your dreams, the Universe will move toward you. Your Higher Self can help, but it won't intrude. Its influence is subtle, gentle, and noninvasive, and it can only be offered if you ask.

Invite your Higher Self to help you—then it can.

PUT YOUR VIBES INTO ACTION

Being aware of your vibes is only part of the process when it comes to living a centered and joy-filled six-sensory life—putting them into action in the world is the other part. When you do so, you place value on your sixth sense, which can then begin to help you in life.

STOP ASKING
FOR OTHERS' OPINIONS

One way to remain true to your authentic self is to stop asking others for their input (unless it's absolutely necessary to do so). Stop soliciting opinions of others, and instead ask your Higher Self for guidance. Remember, it's only when you follow *your* spirit, *your* guidance, *your* heart, and *your* vibes that you can experience true peace of mind. Countless opinions from others will only make it more difficult to hear your higher counsel.

Let your rule be this: "I'll only ask for input if the person I'm asking is wiser, happier, and more balanced that I am." Otherwise, do something completely new—ask your Higher Self instead!

RELEASE THE PAST

As you release yourself from the past, you'll experience a gradual lightening of your soul. You can choose to live in the world guided by your Higher Self and God.

This is a world of spiritual peace and creative expression, one in which you're a vict*or* instead of a vict*im*. You stop living by the old limitations and create a set of new rules. Then, as you remember who you are and start to live by that integrity, your new rules will evolve naturally.

THANK GOD

Try this! Every morning, upon awakening, thank God for a new day and begin it by praying:

Divine Mother, Father God, Higher Self, guides, and angels, lead me this day to the highest degree of awareness and creativity, and to my best possible good. Surprise me—I'm open to miracles!

ALIGN
WITH THE UNIVERSE

When you expect your Higher Self to guide you, you place your full attention, both conscious and subconscious, directly on your Higher Self. This shifts your attention off of other people trying to run your life, and places your power in the hands of the Divine. By making this decision, you become a person who responds to life, rather than one who reacts to it.

Expecting Divine assistance realigns you with God and the Universe at all times. Trusting your vibes to guide you will help you attract all you need to succeed.

BE EXTRAORDINARY

As you embrace the six-sensory life, you'll soon realize that you're becoming a different kind of person: an *extraordinary* person. By shifting your emphasis away from your fears and onto your heart and your Higher Self, life gets easier and easier: The more you listen to your inner voice, the greater the possibility for your personal happiness; and the more you agree to be helped, the more you help the planet. If you're spiritually peaceful, you can touch other people's lives in a positive way, and the healing effect increases. The more light you receive from the spiritual plane, the more you throw out!

You're now leaving the land of the wounded and becoming a bearer of light, a true healer in this world.

DON'T TAKE THINGS PERSONALLY

The more you recognize how powerful you are as a six-sensory being, the more you'll notice doors opening up to you. One way to see this truth more readily is to stop viewing everything from an emotional point of view. Not everything in life is personal—many things just *are*. The more you observe conditions and people with objectivity and detachment, the more insight you'll gain into what to do.

Don't take the behavior of those around you personally. Tell yourself, "It's not my problem!"

BE PATIENT

Be patient and trust your vibes, especially when their advice appears to inconvenience you or upset your plans. Keep an open mind, maintain humor and flexibility when it comes to your intuition—and use your imagination to follow its guidance. It's okay to be nervous at times, as long as you don't ignore what you're feeling.

QUIET
YOUR NERVOUS SYSTEM

Quieting your nervous system and nurturing yourself can save you hours of wasted anxiety, sudden blowups, potential confrontations, health stress, and costly oversights. It's tonic for the spirit!

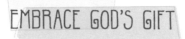

EMBRACE GOD'S GIFT

Your intuition is God's gift to you. It's the collective voice of your Higher Self, your guides, your angels, your teachers, and the Divine. Embrace this gift, and have it work for you by *listening to it!*

Accept that your sixth sense is there to help you, and recognize that it's natural. It will guide, instruct, inspire, lead, and support you . . . if you allow it. It's a loving and beautiful force, but it's also gentle—it won't interfere with you in any way. It's a sacred gift, one you have to choose to accept. If you do, you'll find your life instantly becoming more magical and blessed than ever before.

FOLLOW
YOUR SIXTH SENSE

Often people worry that following their vibes isn't "practical"—it's reckless and irresponsible and could lead to terrible mistakes. Actually, nothing could be further from the truth. Not only is your intuition practical, it's using common sense of the highest order.

Following your sixth sense saves you time, steers you from the wrong path, improves your health, connects you to supportive people, and leads you to your heart's desire and true purpose in life. In fact, it's only through your intuition that you'll experience such peace of mind. Given all that, it's highly impractical *not* to trust your vibes!

KNOW THAT
HIGHER GUIDANCE HEALS

The best part about following your heart and listening to your vibes is that the benefit doesn't stop with you—every life you touch will also be helped.

The loving vibration that comes from following Higher Guidance is contagious. It's calming, grounding, healing, and inspiring; and it attracts great success. And the more guided, peaceful, and happy you are, the more permission you offer others to be the same. The benefits flow out like ripples on the water.

STATE YOUR INTENTIONS

Whatever you want to create, it will be far easier to succeed if you trust your vibes along the way. To jump-start your six-sensory life, tell your subconscious mind that you intend to listen to your intuition starting right now.

The best way to communicate this intention to your subconscious mind is through gentle repetitive suggestions. Here are four basic intentions to get things rolling along:

1. "I am open to my vibes guiding me at all times."

2. "I expect my vibes to actively and accurately guide me in everything."

3. "I trust the vibes that I do get."

4. "I act on my vibes without hesitation."

BE LIGHTHEARTED

As you choose to trust your vibes in life, it's important to be both lighthearted and serious in your commitment.

Remember to see the humor behind all things—lighten up and don't take yourself or anything you face too seriously, but do take your *vibes* seriously. The rewards of making these choices will soon be felt.

SIMPLY LISTEN

Listening to your vibes is an art, and it takes practice. Practice listening to your vibes by . . . simply listening. Just for today, when people speak to you, give them your full and undivided attention. And before you respond, listen to your heart and give *it* your full and undivided attention. Doing so will open all kinds of new avenues, both to others and to your spirit.

LIGHTEN UP!

While you're "clearing out," make sure that you do so on all levels—that is, simplify and purge your life of all that's *emotionally* unnecessary as well. Identify what's yanking on your attention because of neglect, and clean it up! Take care of old business so that you can be free to move on to *new* business.

Let go and complete the past so that your soul can lead you forward.

❀

BE AWARE
OF THE "LITTLE DEALS"

It doesn't have to be a big deal to follow your intuition. In fact, intuition rarely *is* a big deal—it's more often a series of unending "little deals" that make life easier and more magical.

What favorite intuitive "little deals" have you experienced lately?

USE YOUR IMAGINATION

The most direct way to access your intuition is to use your imagination.

Imagination is the front door to your vibes—it creates the world! Not only is it the source of your six-sensory ability, it's the source of *all* your ability.

- "Am I open to allowing my intuition to help me create what I really want?"

- "Can I expect that my intuition will be available to me as I need it?"

- "When I do hear my intuition, am I willing to listen?"

- "Am I willing to ask for guidance in advance?"

- "Am I willing to allow my life to become easier?"

WAKE UP YOUR SPIRIT

The easiest way to trust your vibes is to wake up your spirit. This means getting out of your head and being receptive to all the Divine assistance you have available from higher planes. Don't get stuck in a five-sensory way of life, focused on the ego and based in fear. Instead, step out of the box and begin living the six-sensory life today, focused on your creative purpose and your authentic expression.

Trust your vibes—it's the way to an extraordinary life!

TRUST YOURSELF

When it comes to trusting your vibes, being "right" shouldn't be your absolute goal, especially when you're just beginning to become more sensitive to subtle psychic energy. Accurately picking up on energy is a refined skill that develops with lots of practice—and lots of errors—if you're to become good at it.

If you pick up troubling vibes, yet nothing seems amiss, don't be so sure that you were off. You may be tuning in to a precarious moment where real danger or imbalance does exist, but the situation may correct itself somehow before it evolves into a real or more serious problem. After all, energy, like life, isn't fixed—it's always in a state of motion.

MAKE A NOTE OF IT

One of the more effective ways to tune in to your vibes and let them guide your life is to carry around a little pocket notebook or tape recorder. Every time you feel any little hint, twinge, vibe, or subtle notion, rather than mulling it over and wondering whether or not it's valid (or ignoring it altogether), simply notice the "vibe" and write it down or record it.

Writing down or recording these feelings will accomplish some important things: First, it tells your subconscious mind that you now intend to notice and value your "vibes"; and second, it frees you from the temptation to ignore your intuition. Writing down your perceptions clears your mind, and if done regularly, it will provide you with insight on what disturbs your peace and what ushers it in.

DISPELLING "BAD" VIBES

Sometimes people experience what I call "bad vibes," which cause them to feel worried or anxious. If you feel such negative energy settling over you—for whatever reason—you can do this exercise to restore healing and balance:

First, take a few slow, relaxing breaths, in through the nose and out through the mouth. Next, focus your full attention on the center of your heart, and surround yourself with a golden-white light. Then acknowledge three things that you love about yourself. As you do so, feel this flow of self-love and acceptance moving throughout your entire energy field.

Now if you know the source of your bad vibes, imagine it being surrounded by white light, too. If you don't know the source, ask Divine Spirit to surround the unknown problem and remove it from your energy field. See yourself completely engulfed in love—appreciating, healing, calming, and balancing your vibration. Do this for two or three minutes.

When you're finished, open your eyes.

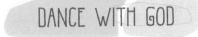

DANCE WITH GOD

Following your vibes is like dancing with God: As you move toward your soul, your soul and the Universe will move toward you!

🌼

CALL ON YOUR GUIDES

Whatever your intentions, you have spiritual helpers called "guides" to help you achieve them. They're there to inspire you, give you bright ideas, offer solutions to problems, attract your attention to opportunity, and work with you to bring about success.

You have guides for many different things, each one devoted to helping you create the best possible human experience you can imagine! The number of helper guides you have working with you changes, depending on what you're doing and how spiritually relevant it is.

Another great way to access higher energy is through your imagination. By using mental imagery, you shift your focus away from the five-sensory world of fear and negative appearances and place it in the creative world of possibilities, solutions, ideas, and answers.

Your imagination is the magic-carpet ride to your new hopes and dreams: Use it to access guidance anytime you need it, ask for direction and inspiration, and lead you to your heart's desire. If you can't imagine it, you can't create it. Imagination is not only the source of your psychic ability, it's the source of *all* your ability!

KNOW THAT YOU HAVE . . .

- **angels**—to protect you,

- **runners**—to help you find things,

- **healers**—to keep you sound,

- **helpers**—to guide you in new projects,

- **teachers**—to help you grow in spirit,

- **joy guides**—to make you laugh, and

- **master guides**—to lead you to your path and purpose in life.

GET TO KNOW YOUR GUIDES

Your guides lovingly seek to serve you . . . be aware of them.

Talk to your guides—don't be shy! Give them names, or ask them what their names are. You'll be surprised by what they tell you. Ask your guides for assistance in every way that you need help. Remember that they *want* to give you their aid.

LET YOUR GUIDES HELP

With your guides' help, life will become even more magical:

- Your days will turn into adventures.

- Loneliness and isolation will disappear.

- Suddenly you'll be surrounded by love.

- You'll attract your heart's desire.

- Life will be full of synchronicities.

- Miracles will happen every day.

HAVE FUN
WITH YOUR GUIDES

Your joy guides are especially fun. These are childlike essences whose purpose is to make you laugh, to invite you to play, and to encourage you to express yourself without self-consciousness. They twinkle past you all the time, trying to engage the kid in you. They lighten you up, free your spirit, and amuse you.

THINGS TO ASK
OF YOUR JOY GUIDES

Can you make me laugh when . . .

. . . I'm feeling depressed?
. . . I'm feeling grief?
. . . I'm feeling afraid?
. . . I'm feeling rejected?
. . . I'm feeling blocked?
. . . I'm feeling drained?
. . . I'm feeling overwhelmed?
. . . I'm feeling that I'm missing
    the point?
. . . I'm causing trouble?
. . . I need to be stopped?
. . . I need some air?

Please help me express my . . .

. . . creativity.
. . . playfulness.
. . . humor.
. . . silliness.
. . . joy.

DO SOMETHING DIFFERENT

If you want to create something new, you must do something different— if you don't, you'll keep getting the same old results.

Right now do something *really* different and give yourself permission to be absolutely psychic in creating your heart's desire. Imagine that you really are that brilliant and inspired. The way to do this is unbelievably easy: All you have to do is pretend that you're psychic!

Imagine that you're an intuitive genius and that you have access to all you need to know about anything at any time. It may sound silly to play this game, but don't underestimate what you can discover. You'll be amazed by how accurate your vibes really are!

SHUT OFF MIND CHATTER

The greatest benefit to training yourself to shut off your mind chatter through meditation is that you slowly get in the habit of listening for the voice of your Higher Self. You'll come to enjoy the relief you get from the endless drone of voices running through your brain.

Through meditation, you'll learn to distinguish the voice of your Higher Self from other voices in your mind. The voice of intuition is subtle, consistent, and calming—and it will show you how to create new beginnings. Listen to it and you'll always feel satisfied!

MEDITATE

Meditation is quite simply the art of relaxing your body and quieting your mind. Training your mind to be still is like training a puppy to sit: The mind likes to jump around and needs to be told many times in a firm but friendly tone to sit still.

Meditation is learning to still your thoughts for about 15 minutes. When you quiet your mind, you break up old mental patterns, open up your awareness, and allow your soul to speak to you.

CONCENTRATE ON YOUR BREATH

Begin meditation by concentrating on your breath. . . .

Start by taking a slow, deep breath. Notice how much aware-ness expands by taking in a single deep breath and then exhaling. This simple act stretches the boundaries of your world a little farther than you're accustomed to and creates room for something totally new.

Next, inhale to the count of four. Hold to the count of four. Exhale to the count of four. Then inhale again and hold to the count of four, and so on. Continue this until you arrive at a comfortable and natural rhythm. You can make this even easier by listening to baroque music as you meditate— its even tempo will synchronize with your breathing and help create the quiet you desire.

Enjoy this for about 15 minutes. Then go on about your day.

FEEL THE BENEFITS

Meditating will make your new six-sensory goal much easier to attain. After only one week of this practice, you'll be able to feel the benefits. Try it and see for yourself!

Be practical—choose a time each day that will accommodate you, and find a quiet place. You may have to overcome stubborn conditioning that suggests that self-care is selfish. It isn't. Self-care is self-*loving*. It will heal you—and it will open you up to loving others instead of being secretly needy and manipulative. Self-care is wise, and it will change your life.

When you feel peaceful and guided, your life will unfold in a whole new way. You'll attract positive people and situations, and life will take on a balanced and inspired quality.

BE CONSISTENT

The best way to assure successful deep meditation is to be consistent. It's far more effective to meditate every day at the same time for 15 minutes than randomly once a week for an hour.

Of course, a busy schedule does make it tricky to find the opportunity to consistently meditate, so you'll have to select a time that works best for you. Try meditating in the morning upon waking and before getting out of bed, or maybe in the evening or after work would be even better. Only you know your schedule and its demands.

Choose a time that's best suited for you, and keep that appointment with your soul.

TRY THE "I AM CALM" TECHNIQUE

This technique always works wonders when you need a break: Simply touch your thumb and forefinger together, take in a deep breath, and quietly say, "I am" as you inhale, and "calm" as you exhale. Allow that feeling of calm to reverberate throughout your entire body.

The act of touching thumb to forefinger will serve as a physical reminder to come back to the moment, and actually vocalizing "I am calm" will wash away your stress!

GUESS WHAT?

Meditation isn't another thing "to do"—it's an invitation to *stop* "doing."

JUST ASK

God cares for you so much that He provides you with love, protection, safety, inspiration, ideas, solutions, and everything else you need to grow and thrive in life. And the Universe is ready, willing, and able to assist you—but before it can, *you need to ask the Universe for help and guidance.*

Why not try it today?

PRAY

The most direct way to ask for help is to pray. And one of the most powerful ways to do so is to be thankful for what you have right now. Gratitude affects our consciousness in the same way that windshield wipers affect our car's windows in a blizzard: It clears away confusion and helps us see the world more clearly.

Practicing gratitude as a form of prayer is very easy . . . and immediately rewarding. All you need to do is acknowledge and thank the Universe for all your blessings, whether they come in the form of good health, loving family members, close friends, or simply being alive. Do this often.

BE WILLING TO BE HELPED

Know that your guides can't help you unless you invite them to. When you ask for their aid, you give them permission to assist you in every possible way.

Get in the habit of asking for guidance all the time. Your willingness to be assisted by your guides also helps the planet: As you achieve more balance, you contribute more balance to the earth.

ACT ON YOUR VIBES

Do something different and act on your vibes without hesitation! Take that leap of faith and propel your soul forward into the world of the extraordinary. Every time you choose to instantly act on your intuition, you release yourself from living your life through the limited power of your ego and place the power of your life into the hands of your soul—and into the hands of the Divine.

Acting on your intuition is making the choice to allow your life to be directed from a Divine source, as opposed to being directed by your fears. When you follow your vibes, you enter a brand-new world—one that aspires to assist you in every possible way.

Have your acted on your vibes today? How?

RESIGN FROM THE CLUB

Just for today, resign from the "shoulda, woulda, coulda" club of missed opportunity and ignored intuition. Your vibes are there to help you—let them work for you instead of you working against them.

FOCUS ON THE ESSENCE

Trusting your vibes is actually the art and practice of listening with your heart, for it is there that the voice of inner wisdom speaks, influencing the way we take in information.

Listening from the heart helps us focus on becoming aware of not only the *content* of information but its *intent,* or essence, as well.

STAY GROUNDED

Keeping yourself grounded will greatly enhance your ability to tune in to your vibes. Try it!

When you're grounded and clear, you may find that you're more energetic, your mood lifts, and you're more open and aware—which is the perfect state for receiving higher guidance. When you're bogged down with other people's negative energy, however, it's like looking through dirty windows in an electrical storm. In such a state, you can't remain true to your path or your goals.

GET OUT OF YOUR HEAD

Anytime you get "out of your head" and "into your body," you become more grounded—just as you do whenever you use your hands or engage in a physical activity.

Here are some useful ways to attain this state:

- Exercise.
- Cook.
- Give yourself a foot massage.
- Work with clay.
- Break bread.
- Clean a closet.
- Fold the laundry.
- Lie on the ground.
- Look at the stars.
- Play sports.
- Dance to your favorite music.
- Drum on anything.

FLEX YOUR FEET

Here's another great grounding exercise:

> *Sit comfortably in a chair and remove your socks and shoes. Flex your ankles and feet until they feel loose and relaxed.*
>
> *Place one foot at a time in your lap and give yourself a foot massage—paying close attention to the ankle, the toes, the arch, and even the calf. Use peppermint lotion to enhance the experience. Notice how relaxed and grounded you begin to feel while doing this. The more you massage, the more centered you become*
>
> *Five minutes will work miracles anytime you're anxious, worried, overextended, or fatigued and need a boost.*

STAY GROUNDED

How often should you get grounded? As often as necessary. Do it until it becomes second nature—until you become used to being grounded as a natural state.

A grounded state is a peaceful, effective, and healing one. It keeps you open to new solutions, possibilities, and opportunities. It will prevent you from falling backward into anyone's negative energy trap. Being grounded enables you to continually go forward, moving toward what you really want in life.

✿

CLEAR THE PAST

If you want to create something new, you must first clear away the past. You can't move into new conditions if you don't first release yourself from the old ones. This includes negative feelings you may hold toward those who have hurt you or caused you to suffer. It also includes releasing yourself from all resentment, anger, and self-abuse that keeps you from experiencing a loving life in the moment.

Observe your life, knowing that the more complex and difficult it's been, the more opportunity there's been for your soul's growth. See your past as part of your spiritual tests—some of which you passed the first time around, while others take more time.

The best way to release the past is to forgive all that has transpired in it. This includes forgiving yourself as well as anyone else who has hurt you.

LIGHTEN THE LOAD

Recognize what's tugging on your attention because of neglect or procrastination—and clean it up so that your soul can get on with more important things.

If you're entering a six-sensory life, you have to travel lightly. Ask yourself whether you're holding on to:

- unnecessary baggage from the past,

- unfinished business in the present, or

- self-sabotaging fears about the future.

SLOW DOWN

As you release yourself from the past and clear the way for new beginnings, life begins to take on wonder and excitement.

Notice the beauty of being in the moment: Slow down, breathe, and pay attention to the miraculous world you live in today. Make a point to actually notice where you are right now, using all your senses. What do you see? What do you hear? What do you smell? What do you feel?

Where are you now? And where do you want to go next?

LET GO

"Letting go" does not come easily.

It takes practice to let go of the old and reach for something new. Today, practice letting go of fear and listening to your heart. Pay attention to what it tells you . . . and check in with it often.

GET ORGANIZED

Get organized! Doing so will unclog the drains in your life and clean out energy wasters, allowing new and more exciting positive energy to flow.

WHAT DO
YOU CARE ABOUT?

Organization follows your true intentions, or what you really care about in your life.

Start by organizing your true soul goals, and write down your intentions. What do you care about? What's the most important thing in your life right now? What are you willing to commit to?

Organize your time and awareness around these absolutely essential goals.

SIMPLIFY

Disorganization is both an energy leak *and* drain. Look at your physical surroundings and notice whether or not they reflect order, balance, and commitment to what's most important to you now. The more you have order on the outside, the more you can have order within.

This means that it's time to let go of the unnecessary. Clear the way for new things to come in by purging the old! Eliminate all the unnecessary, outdated, useless stuff blocking the path for your new life to emerge. If something no longer serves you, donate it to the Universe.

Simplify. Lighten up. Make way for the new.

BREATHE INTO FEAR

If you want to move toward your dreams, don't be attached to your fears!

Don't burden yourself with useless notions, secondhand opinions, or reality as other people see it. The Universe doesn't favor one goal over another in creating what you really want—it does, however, employ synchronicity and grace. If you follow your heart and listen to your intuition, you'll receive these gifts along the way.

Remember, when you breathe into fear, it turns into adventure. The greater the fear, the bigger the adventure.

What are your greatest fears right now?

ASK YOURSELF . . .

- "What old business is holding me back?"

- "What baggage must I let go of?"

- "What fears are dragging me down?"

LEAD FROM YOUR SOUL

Lead from your soul—not from fear.

Leading from fear is like driving a car with the emergency brake on: It's awkward. But leading from your vibes is like being driven by a chauffeur . . . in a Rolls-Royce.

ACCEPT FEAR—
DON'T LET IT STOP YOU

Often people say, "I want a change, but I'm afraid that I'll make a mistake." Being afraid is normal when it comes to trying something new.

Don't wait for your fear to go away—simply accept it as part of being human, and follow your heart and your intuition anyway.

And know that it isn't your fear that stops you—*hiding* it is what saps your energy. Accept fear as a part of being human—don't let it stop you.

What are you afraid of?

ASK FOR HELP

One of the easiest ways to ask the Universe to support you is to close your eyes, think of your problem or challenge, and then say . . . *"Help!"*

REMEMBER . . .

. . . ask the Universe for help, but don't tell it *how* to help you.

KNOW THAT IT JUST GETS BETTER

Joy is a landmark of the six-sensory life!

Know that you're now being helped in more ways than you could possibly imagine. Count the myriad blessings pouring upon you with every subtle twist, magical moment, intense impulse, and bright idea that comes your way each day.

And guess what? It only gets better from here.

DISCOVER
YOUR AUTHENTIC SELF

Your sixth sense is the guiding voice of your soul, and a natural and important part of who you are. Without it you can't find your way to your purpose and path in life—and you certainly can't truly discover what brings you authentic joy.

FOUR WAYS TO INVITE MORE JOY INTO YOUR LIFE

1. Be open to six-sensory guidance every day.

2. Expect intuitive help on everything, at every moment.

3. Trust your vibes when you get them.

4. Act on your sixth sense instead of ignoring it.

WALK IT OFF

Nothing restores you to your natural state of inner joy more effectively than a walk in nature. This is so effective for aura balancing that you may want to incorporate a short walk into your daily routine just as an insurance policy for health and happiness.

Even twice around the block will be sufficient to drain away interference, eliminate psychic pollution, and restore clarity.

REMEMBER TO LAUGH

My mother always said, "Remember to laugh. The situation may be critical, but it's never serious."

THINK ABOUT THIS . . .

What's the most critical situation you face right now? And what's humorous about it?

PLAY THE ARTFUL DODGER

Become conscious of how people affect you. When you're unaware of this, you may not notice yourself feeling drained, or you may become cranky with the next person down the line just to expel your acquired negativity.

Once you become cognizant of how people affect you, make a whole new set of choices. Learn to *observe,* not *absorb,* negativity from others—this will help you remain faithful to what's now important to you, instead of being thrown off course.

Play the artful dodger, and avoid negative traps.

FILL IN THE BLANK:

If I wasn't afraid, I would _____

_____

_____

_____

Listen to the answer, for that's the voice of your soul. Follow it!

GET RID OF IT!

The first and most obvious way to create a calm and peaceful sacred space in your home is to keep it clean and organized and filled with beautiful things that comfort your spirit.

Everything is comprised of energy, and everything you own absorbs your vibrations. The same holds true for negative energy—it will also linger in an atmosphere, bringing you down with its dreary and brittle vibes. That's why if you live in messy, unloved, and neglected disarray, you'll come to resent it. First, the ugly environment itself discharges negative energy, and the resentment you feel because of it keeps recycling those dark feelings.

The best cure for this problem is to clean and clear out all that isn't necessary or soothing to your spirit. If it's ugly, irritating, broken-down, or useless—or if it reminds you of something or someone unpleasant—get rid of it! Given the effect it has on you, it isn't worth keeping.

BEAUTIFY YOUR SURROUNDINGS

The human spirit thrives on harmony, beauty, and balance. My spiritual teachers taught me that this is essential to our soul's happiness—it's not an option.

Bring this energy into your life: Paint your home in tranquil tones. Bring in fresh flowers. Arrange your furniture in pleasant arrangements. Eliminate clutter and disorder. Burn incense. Hang beautiful art and mirrors to enhance the light. Open the blinds and shades and let the sunshine in. And if your home is naturally dark, hang mirrors and burn full-spectrum lightbulbs to brighten it up. Light keeps energy moving.

Love yourself enough to care, and create harmony in every room.

BLESS YOUR HOME

First, light a candle. Now walk from room to room, asking Divine Spirit to bless your home:

- As you bless the living room, ask Divine Spirit to bring you pleasant company and positive memories.

- As you bless the kitchen, ask Divine Spirit to nurture your body and soul.

- As you bless the bedroom, ask Divine Spirit to soothe and heal you as you sleep, and to bring you pleasant dreams.

- Thank God in your own way for providing you with a safe haven and peaceful sanctuary. Ask for continued protection and blessings in your home.

(You can also do this whenever you travel and find yourself sleeping in another space.)

CREATE A SACRED ALTAR

A wonderful way to create a healing vibration in your home is to create a sacred altar. Set it up in a corner of your home where it will be left undisturbed, such as on a small table or dresser. (It can even be set up on the floor if it won't be in the way.)

On your altar, place your most beloved objects, photos, and talismans, representing those people and things that you love. You may also want to place fresh flowers, candles, or incense upon it. And you might include religious icons, family photos, even articles from nature—anything that lifts your spirits and moves you into your heart space.

Let your altar serve as a site for contemplation, reverie, meditation, and prayer. Eventually this sacred spot will become charged with the vibration of peace and tranquility, and it will serve as a healing place for you.

LISTEN TO MUSIC

Listen to calming, meditative, or classical music to keep you clear, centered, and peaceful. The minute you hear music, your awareness leaves your head and moves into your heart.

It's a known fact that Baroque music—especially Bach, Vivaldi, Telemann, or Handel—calms the heartbeat and creates an inner state of tranquility.

LIVE IN PEACE AND QUIET

Loud and dissonant noises are disturbing to your spirit—so is music with negative lyrics; talk-radio or television shows that spew hateful messages; malicious office or neighborhood gossip; and arguing, fighting, and cursing with anyone in your environment.

To the best of your ability, keep the level and quality of sound, tone, and conversation around you positive and pleasant (this includes the volume of TVs, stereos, and voices). Noise pollution—and thought pollution!—steals away our peace of mind, and we must be watchful for these subtle saboteurs of our inner tranquility.

Be conscious of how delicate you are, and of how your spirit needs harmonious vibes.

SING YOUR HEART OUT!

Did you know that when you dance and sing, your spirit fully enters your body?

To awaken your spirit and fill you with its loving and healing energy, turn up the volume on your favorite song, and sing your heart out until you feel absolutely fabulous!

LAUGH!

We first need to laugh at our mistakes before we can learn from them.

Laughter brings distance, perception, and sometimes insight. It also reminds us that who we are (spiritual beings put here on Earth to create) and what we do (make mistakes) aren't the same thing. Laughter keeps our self-worth intact as it emphasizes the need to look foolish at times to gain discovery.

NOTICE THE WORLD AROUND YOU

Be aware of the world around you, including the energy of others. The more you notice, the better informed you'll be. And then, the better decisions you'll make—ones that will take you to where you really want to go in life. Here's how:

- When interacting with people, study them. Listen to what they're saying and focus on what they mean. Take a deep breath, and note how their energy feels to you.

- Practice sensing the various types of energy each person sends out and how it affects you physically, emotionally, and energetically: Do you feel supported or in harmony with this individual, or does he or she have a negative effect on you?

- Pay attention—don't ignore anything, and let your own experience guide you.

- If you have a positive experience, be open. However, if you feel drained or upset, step away (if possible), and don't let this person drag you down.

This awareness is the beginning of personal empowerment, allowing you to make choices that support your spirit.

SURROUND YOURSELF WITH WHITE LIGHT

As you move toward your intentions, people around *you* may react negatively. Change is scary for everyone, and as *you* change, others may try to stop you. Send them love, but protect yourself from any harmful interference:

> *See yourself surrounded by a golden-white light that deflects all negativity and fear and only allows loving, positive, supportive energy to influence you.*

RENEW CONNECTIONS

Remaining in touch with those you love is vital to your sense of personal joy and well-being. Yet with so many people losing touch in today's fast-paced world, this becomes harder and harder to do. Try the following if you feel disconnected from someone special:

> *Simply focus on your heart and think of the person you're missing. Say his (or her) name to yourself and ask Divine Spirit to surround him with a pure white light of loving protection. Imagine this white light completely covering him wherever he is. See him in you mind's eye as safe, protected, and in total peace. And send*

him your love. While you're at it, include yourself in the blessing as well.

This simple exercise is almost always felt, and often that very person will contact you soon after he feels the good vibes coming his way.

 AND, FINALLY . . .

. . . don't forget to say thank you to the Universe for all the gifts, blessings, and support you receive every day!

ABOUT THE AUTHOR

Sonia Choquette is a world-renowned author, storyteller, vibrational healer, and six-sensory spiritual teacher in international demand for her guidance, wisdom, and capacity to heal the soul. She's the author of eight best-selling books, including *Diary of a Psychic* and *Trust Your Vibes,* and numerous audio editions and card decks. Sonia was educated at the University of Denver, the Sorbonne in Paris, and holds a Ph.D. in metaphysics from the American Institute of Holistic Theology. She resides with her family in Chicago.

Website:
www.soniachoquette.com

NOTES

NOTES

HAY HOUSE TITLES
OF RELATED INTEREST

We hope you enjoyed this Hay House book.
If you'd like to receive a free catalog featuring additional
Hay House books and products, or if you'd like information
about the Hay Foundation, please contact:

Hay House, Inc., P.O. Box 5100
Carlsbad, CA 92018-5100

(760) 431-7695 or **(800) 654-5126**
(760) 431-6948 (fax)
or **(800) 650-5115 (fax)**
www.hayhouse.com

Published and distributed in Australia by:
Hay House Australia Pty. Ltd., 18/36 Ralph St.,
Alexandria NSW 2015 • Phone: 612-9669-4299
Fax: 612-9669-4144 • www.hayhouse.com.au

Published and distributed in the United Kingdom by:
Hay House UK, Ltd., 292B Kensal Rd., London W10 5BE
Phone: 44-20-8962-1230 • Fax: 44-20-8962-1239
www.hayhouse.co.uk

Published and distributed in the Republic of South Africa by:
Hay House SA (Pty), Ltd., P.O. Box 990, Witkoppen 2068
Phone/Fax: 27-11-706-6612 • orders@psdprom.co.za

Published in India by: Hay House Publications (India) Pvt. Ltd.
www.hayhouseindia.co.in

Distributed in India by: Media Star, 7 Vaswani Mansion,
120 Dinshaw Vachha Rd., Churchgate, Mumbai 400020
Phone: 91 (22) 22815538-39-40 • Fax: 91 (22) 22839619
booksdivision@mediastar.co.in

Distributed in Canada by: Raincoast ,
9050 Shaughnessy St., Vancouver, B.C. V6P 6E5
Phone: (604) 323-7100 • Fax: (604) 323-2600 • www.raincoast.com

Tune in to **HayHouseRadio.com**® for the best in inspirational
talk radio featuring top Hay House authors! And, sign up via the
Hay House USA Website to receive the Hay House online newsletter
and stay informed about what's going on with your favorite
authors. You'll receive bimonthly announcements about Discounts
and Offers, Special Events, Product Highlights, Free Excerpts,
Giveaways, and more!
www.hayhouse.com®